A Look at Romans

Lisa-Anne Berry

A Look at Romans

Cover Design: K&J Couture Designs
https://www.behance.net/kjcdesignsme

Thank you to Fayette Baptist Church and
New England Bible College
for providing classes that impact lives.

Thank you to Dr. Samuel Caldwell for
his thorough instruction and passion while teaching
the book of Romans.

Romans 6:23

For the wages of sin is death, but the gracious gift of God is eternal life in Christ Jesus our Lord.

Table of Contents

Introduction

We are called as Christians to know God. Not just to know Him, but to know Him intimately, as a close friend. If you were to think about your closest friend, you would most likely be able to list what they liked and disliked. You would perhaps know their favorite food or their favorite song or maybe their favorite color. You might know about their family and how they interact with them. You probably would want to spend time with them and look forward to doing so.

We are called to have this type of relationship with God. We can't know Him if we don't spend time with Him and learn about what He likes and dislikes. We can do this by reading and studying the Scriptures. Every chapter of the Bible can give us information about God, His likes and dislikes, how we are to interact with others and with Him, how we are to love, and so much more. We just need to look for it.

All scripture is inspired by God and profitable for teaching, for reproof, for correction, for training in righteousness; so that the man of God may be adequate, equipped for every good work.
2 Timothy 3:16-17

Paul, the author of Romans, has shared information about God, how we should interact with Him and what He is like throughout each chapter. Paul is a man who has an intimate relationship with God. He is sharing what he knows, what he believes, and what the Holy Spirit has shared with him.

We often read the Scriptures just to say we have read them. We may skim over the surface instead of diving deeper. It is my hope this study helps you to dive a bit deeper below the surface to know our Father God better than you have before.

How to Use This Study

You may wish to use a separate notebook in addition to a Bible. Any version of the Bible will work, however the scripture quotes in this study are taken from the New American Standard version.

1. Begin by reading each chapter of Romans that corresponds to the chapter in the study. As you read, note the things you discover about God. Either do this by marking them in your Bible or by creating a running list in your notebook. Either way, read slowly and thoughtfully. Notice all the things mentioned about God and His character.

2. Read next the short devotional for each chapter included in this book.

3. Answer the questions at the end of each chapter. Do not skip over them. There is space for your answers included or you can jot down your thoughts in your journal. Dig deep into this study to learn not only more about God but about yourself as you relate to the Almighty One.

4. Write out at least one verse per chapter that stands out to you. This may be a verse which is familiar or one that has a truth about God you don't want to forget.

5. Memorize the verses as you study the book of Romans. We are called to hide God's word in our heart as it says in Psalms 119:11 *"Your word I have treasured* [or hidden] *in my heart, that I may not sin against You."*

Above all, look to Scripture for the answers you seek. God's Word never returns void (see Isaiah 55:11). It is living and breathing and can teach us new truths daily if we simply seek them.

Chapter 1

Paul calls himself a bond-servant of Christ Jesus in the very beginning of chapter one, before he ever says anything else (Romans 1:1). We often have a negative view of what it means to be a servant or a bond-servant. We may think of poor immigrants to the New World or even those living in Europe who were so poor they could not survive on their own. Being a slave for seven years in the hope of a better life was the choice made over facing a certain death. However, a new and better life often didn't happen.

If we are a servant of God, is that a negative thing? We are called to serve God fully and completely. We should *want* to be His bond-servant and serve Him.

When we are fully serving God, we are fully focused on what He is calling us to do, where He is sending us, and all He would have us to learn.

In order to serve God, we must know God. In order to know God, we must study His word. We must pray to have communication with Him. We must be fully committed to wanting to know more about Him.

God is the master over us. If one is a servant, one must have a master, an overseer, or one who directs the path of the servant. God is this for us. He is the one who is directing our path and nudging us (or even pushing us at times) to do His will.

When we know God intimately, we are more likely to follow His direction for us. He is a loving God and wants only the best for us. We would be wise to follow His leading.

Things to Think On:

1. What are your thoughts on being called a bond-servant of Christ?

   _____

   _____

   _____

   _____

   _____

   _____

   _____

   _____

   _____

   _____

   _____

2. Do you feel any negative connotations about this term? If so, why? If not, why not?

   _____

   _____

   _____

   _____

_____

_____

_____

_____

_____

3. Others in the Scriptures were called
    "bond-servants of God or servant of
    God." List a few including the
    references where you found the
    information. BibleGateway.com has a
    search feature that will help you.

    _____

    _____

    _____

    _____

    _____

    _____

    _____

    _____

    _____

_____

_____

_____

4. Write out one verse that stood out to
   you from Romans Chapter 1.

   _____

   _____

   _____

   _____

Chapter 2

While God loves us and wants us to be fully devoted to Him as a bond-servant, He also tells us He will be the final judge of our actions. He isn't, however, a wrathful judge, sitting on His heavenly throne waiting for us mere mortals on earth to mess up in order to zap us into an eternal hell.

While many unbelievers may think this, Romans 2:4 tells us three things about God's attributes we should remember: He is kind, He is tolerant, and He is patient. A God with those types of character traits doesn't want us to fail. He wants us to succeed. Most importantly, He wants us to repent.

In chapter one, we saw how mankind knew God but did not honor Him (Romans 1:21). They created idols to worship instead of worshipping their creator. God *gave them over* to the *lusts of their hearts* (Romans 1:24). We then read a long list of degrading actions mankind ends up following. It seems rather hopeless.

Here in chapter two, we read how God will judge mankind's actions. How can we say then that God loves us? Why would a kind, tolerant, and patient God judge us?

The same way we can say most parents love their children. If there is a loving parent-child relationship and the child is being disobedient, the parent will discipline the child out of love and the desire for the child to do what is right, willingly. God does the same with us. We are, after all, His children. He treats us as such.

We serve a loving God who does not show partiality (Romans 2:11). You cannot talk your way out of trouble with Him or try to gain favor. In verse sixteen of this second chapter of Romans, we read these words:

"…God will judge the secrets of men through Christ Jesus."

People often go through life thinking no one ever sees when they do something wrong, something against God's will. They forget God sees all and knows all. There is no hiding from God.

How then should we live? We should live in accordance with God's will for our lives. The only way to know this is to read God's word, to study it, and to pray.

When we mess up, because we most assuredly will mess up, we must be quick to ask for forgiveness and repent of our sins. We cannot know how we should live if we do not know the things God wants most for us. Living a righteous life before God is what we are called to do. We must do our very best to follow His will for us.

Things to Think On:

1. Do you feel you have been following God's will for your life? Why or why not?

   _____

   _____

   _____

   _____

   _____

   _____

   _____

   _____

2. Have you ever tried to hide something from God? Have you confessed your indiscretion and asked God for forgiveness? Take that opportunity today and write them here.

   _____

   _____

   _____

_____

_____

_____

_____

_____

_____

_____

3. Do you read God's word regularly? If not, now is the time to start. Make a specific plan. The free YouVersion Bible app offers many reading plans.

_____

_____

_____

_____

_____

_____

_____

_____

_____

4. Write out one verse that stood out to you from Romans Chapter 2.

   _____

   _____

   _____

   _____

   _____

   _____

Chapter 3

If there were one word to sum up what chapter three tells us most about God, it would likely be righteousness. But what is righteousness?

We see this word a lot in the Bible and it often refers to God and His character. But do we truly know what it means?

Righteousness, at its root, is simply being and acting right. God sets right from wrong. Acting right, being righteous, means doing things His way.

The Webster 1828 dictionary says this: "*conformity of heart and life to the divine law. It includes all we call justice, honesty, and virtue, with holy affections; in short, it is true religion.*" God is the epitome of this word, as He should be. God has all these attributes: justice, honesty, and virtue.

Let's start with justice. God is just. He is also a justifier or one who pardons one from guilt and punishment (Romans 3:26). As sinners, all people should pay for their sin, but we don't. Jesus took our penalty (Romans 3:24-25). He took the pain and death intended for us instead.

God knew people would fail and people did and have and will continue to do so. Does that mean we should continue in our sin? Not at all! We still need to live for God, which means when we sin, we repent quickly and earnestly. No one can live a perfect life, but one can still live a life for God.

God is also honest (Romans 3:4). God will never lie. What God says He will do, He does. What God promises, He fulfills. He is always truthful. It is us, sinful people, who lie, thinking God will not know the difference. When we view God through the lens of our humanness, we can forget God never fails. Ever.

God is also righteous. All people fail to meet this standard. All people should die for their sins. It doesn't matter if they are a Jew or Gentile (a Jew by birth or any other nation by birth).

Romans 3:10 sums it up nicely, *"There is none righteous, not even one."* We also have Romans 3:23, which states *"for all have sinned and fall short of the glory of God."* How then can we ever think to live up to God's righteous standards?

Simply put, we cannot. What we can do is remember God is faithful and true. When we come to Him and repent of our sins, He will forgive them. He wants nothing more than to see us walk in the truth of His word.

Things to Think On:

1. Does it help or hinder you to think of trying to live up to a perfect God?

    _____

    _____

    _____

    _____

    _____

    _____

    _____

    _____

    _____

2. What attributes of God in chapter three give you the most comfort? Why?

    _____

    _____

    _____

    _____

    _____

_____

_____

_____

_____

_____

3. How will you live differently knowing
   that God will one day judge you?

   _____

   _____

   _____

   _____

   _____

   _____

   _____

   _____

   _____

   _____

   _____

   _____

4. Write out one verse that stood out to you from Romans Chapter 3.

    _____

    _____

    _____

    _____

    _____

    _____

Chapter 4

Many faithful people lived before Jesus came to earth. This means many people died before Jesus' death and resurrection made the way for salvation. These people lived under the Law, the Law given to Moses and passed on to the nation of Israel by God. How then were these people saved? When they died, what happened to them? Did they go to heaven?

Faith is an important aspect of justification. But first, let's define justification since this word is used often throughout Scripture. Justification is defined in the Webster 1828 dictionary as "...*remission of sin and absolution from guilt and punishment; or an act of free grace by which God pardons the sinner and accepts him as righteous, on account of the atonement of Christ.*" So, how then are these Old

Testament believers justified? Christ had not yet atoned or paid for their sins.

God always has a plan. As we have already learned: He is our master, He loves us, He is our judge, He is kind, He is tolerant, He is patient, He is righteous, He is just, He is honest, and He is virtuous. That is a lot for so few chapters in one book of the Bible.

Rest assured. He had a plan set up all along for the believers that lived before Christ. The key to their salvation was simply faith. Romans 4:3 and Genesis 15:6 state why these believers will have the same eternal fate as those who came after Christ – their faith. *"Abraham believed God and it was credited to him as righteousness."* (Romans 4:3) They believed God. How simple and yet profound.

Abraham was not saved by his works but by his faith (Romans 4:2). We must have faith in God. Faith He will do all He says He will do. We need to remember God always fulfills His promises to us (Romans 4:21). We must be faithful to believe in Him and to follow His plan for us.

Things to Think On:

1. What attribute of God has surprised you the most at this point? Why?

   _____

   _____

   _____

   _____

   _____

   _____

   _____

   _____

   _____

2. Have you ever thought about how Old Testament people were saved? Does anything you have learned today match with what you believed about this?

   _____

   _____

   _____

   _____

_____

_____

_____

_____

_____

3. How important is your faith to you?
   Explain your answer.

_____

_____

_____

_____

_____

_____

_____

_____

_____

_____

_____

_____

4. Write out one verse that stood out to you from Romans Chapter 4.

_____

_____

_____

_____

_____

_____

Chapter 5

Many people know John 3:16, *"For God so loved the world, that He gave His only Son, so that everyone who believes in Him will not perish, but have eternal life."* God loves us. He loves you. He loves me. He loves your enemy. He loves your neighbor. He loves everyone. He pours out this love to us through the Holy Spirit (Romans 5:5).

We are not promised a loving, pain-free existence, however. In fact, we are told to *"exult in our tribulations"* in Romans 5:3. But remember, God always has a reason for everything He tells us to do.

So, why should we exult or rejoice exceedingly in our tribulations? Paul tells us why in Romans chapter five verses three to five. We rejoice in our tribulations because it will bring about a steady course of action (following God) amid difficulty.

When we persevere like that, we begin to build our character. When we have proved our character (built it), we have hope. Why is this important? Because hope never disappoints since the love of God has been poured out into our hearts by the Holy Spirit.

Our faith in God makes us right with God, which gives us peace with God. God never promised us an easy life. In fact, we are told a life following Christ will be difficult. Even Paul had difficulty. But the difficulty is worth it because of the end result.

And what is the result? It is eternal life with Christ free of pain and difficulty. A moment of pain and difficulty on earth exchanged for an eternal lifetime of peace and joy with God. It seems a willing price to pay.

Things to Think On:

1. Do you feel as if you have a better grasp on what it means to live for God? What does this look like specifically in your life?

_____

_____

_____

_____

_____

_____

_____

_____

_____

_____

_____

_____

_____

_____

_____

_____

2. What changes can you make today to do better?

_____

_____

_____

_____

_____

_____

_____

3. How has God blessed your life? Make sure to look through the difficult times to see where He came along beside you to help. Journal about His faithfulness.

_____

_____

_____

_____

_____

_____

_____

_____

_____

_____

_____

_____

_____

4. Write out one verse that stood out to
   you from Romans Chapter 5.

   _____

   _____

   _____

   _____

   _____

Chapter 6

Christ came to earth as the Son of God for one purpose – to save people from their sins. Ever since Adam and Eve lived, sin and death have reigned here on earth. Though he knew in advance it would happen, sin was never God's intention.

God always intended for mankind to live with Him forever. He had to make a way for that to happen through the man of Jesus Christ, His Son whom He sent to earth in order to fulfill His ultimate plan.

The sixth chapter of Romans is about this very issue. Christ suffered and died in order to take on all the sins of all the people who have ever lived, before His birth, during His time here on earth, and long after He was dead. How humbling this thought should be!

Christ's death had to happen. It was the only way people would be able to be reconciled to God. Now that it has been completed, it never has to happen again. Christ is alive today and will remain so forever (Romans 6:9). His death occurred in order for sin to lose its grip on the world (Romans 6:10).

This amazing thought works both ways. Because Christ died for the sins of all people, because He took the sins of everyone on Himself, we are also dead to sin but alive in God (Romans 6:11).

We are alive currently here on earth, yes, but we will one day be alive in heaven. We will live with Christ forever. This would not have been possible without His sacrifice. This gift of eternal life is immediately available for the taking (Romans 8:23). Now that is truly an amazing thought!

Things to Think On:

1. God gives us His grace freely and
    without hesitation. Does this mean
    we can continue to sin? Make sure to
    focus on Romans 6:1-2 for the
    answer.

    _____

    _____

    _____

    _____

    _____

    _____

    _____

    _____

    _____

    _____

    _____

    _____

    _____

    _____

    _____

2. Our focus should be on God and not sin. What sins in your life are you focused on lately? How can you change your focus to be more heavenly directed?

_____

_____

_____

_____

_____

_____

_____

_____

_____

_____

_____

_____

_____

_____

_____

_____

_____

3. When we look at all the laws in the Old Testament what feeling do you think the Israelites might have had from trying *not* break any of them? Then look at what Romans is telling us about grace? How is that different? Which one would be easier to live with? Is there any area of your life in which you are continuing to try to follow the Law instead of living in the grace of God?

_____

_____

_____

_____

_____

_____

_____

_____

_____

_____

_____

_____

_____

_____

_____

_____

_____

_____

4. Write out one verse that stood out to you from Romans Chapter 6.

_____

_____

_____

_____

_____

Chapter 7

At the end of the last chapter, you were asked to take a look at how the Old Testament laws compared to New Testament grace. Let's delve into that a bit more here.

By the time Christ started His ministry here on earth, the Jewish leaders had created so many laws for their people to follow they were sinning daily if not hourly. It was impossible to live a life free of sin. The only way people can live a life without sin is to obey God, and even then it's impossible without constant forgiveness. The laws were so numerous it was impossible to obey them all the time. Thus, people sinned constantly.

That was the whole point.

God needed the people to realize the importance of Jesus' death on the cross. Christ's death helped the Jewish people die to the Law (Romans 7:4). It had served its purpose. The Law had pointed out throughout the ages how impossible it was to follow, to be free from sin, to live for God one hundred percent of the time.

Christ changed everything forever when He willingly allowed Himself to be sacrificed on the cross for each one of us, not just the Jews. By being a sinless man taking on the sins of the entire world for all eternity, Christ did what the Law could never do. He gave people eternal life, a life that can never be lost.

Instead all people, not just the Jews, were raised to life *with* Christ. We were joined with Him for all of eternity. You didn't have to be born a Jew. You didn't have to follow all the laws given to Moses. You simply needed to believe Christ died for your sins and rose again on the third day.

God had the perfect reason for this. Yes, He wanted to ensure eternal life for all willing people. However, He also wanted all those who were raised to life with Christ to also bear fruit for God.

Bearing fruit in our life means we live a life that points towards God. Our actions, our words, our deeds, all of these things point directly to God.

The laws were in place to show people's inability to save themselves. Christ came to set them free from sin. Without Him, it was impossible. With Him, we are free from sin's death grip.

Things to Think On:

1. Examine your life. How do you show the fruit of God in it? List 3-5 ways you do this.   If this is hard for you, ask a friend or loved one to help you see God's fruit in your life.

_____

_____

_____

_____

_____

_____

_____

_____

_____

_____

_____

_____

_____

_____

2. If God wants us to follow Christ and His teachings, does it mean we are free from having to follow things like the 10 Commandments? Why or why not?

_____

_____

_____

_____

_____

_____

_____

_____

_____

_____

_____

_____

_____

_____

_____

3. It would seem in reading Romans 7:15-20 that we are hopelessly caught in sin's trap. What can free us and give us hope?

_____

_____

_____

_____

_____

_____

_____

_____

_____

4. Write out one verse that stood out to you from Romans Chapter 7.

_____

_____

_____

_____

_____

Chapter 8

Our lives can often seem hopeless. We may feel caught in a cycle of sin we cannot seem to break. And yet, there is a way out.

Read Romans 8:1 out loud to yourself. *"Therefore there is now no condemnation at all for those who are in Christ Jesus."* Now do it again. Do you believe this? One of the things Paul tells us again and again in this chapter of Romans is that Christ does not condemn us. This means even though we sin, even though life appears hopeless, all it will take is one simple prayer asking for forgiveness and all is restored.

That can sometimes be hard to believe. "After all I have done" …. fill in the blank." We then think there is no way Christ will ever forgive us of whatever it is we have done.

My dear one, if you still feel this way, please re-read this chapter again and again and again. It is full of the words of God saying the exact opposite. He *will* free you of the guilt holding you hostage. There is nothing you have done He won't forgive. If you still need some convincing, read Psalm 103 and focus on verse twelve.

God sent His only Son to earth as a sacrifice for you. He would have still done it if you were the only person on earth to save.

The thoughts and feelings of being impossible to forgive aren't from Christ. They are from the evil one. The one who wants us to fail. The one who doesn't want us to see the free gift Christ offers.

The best thing we can do is stay focused on Christ. To do this, we must allow the Holy Spirit to rule our lives. The Spirit will help keep us focused on a life of peace instead of death (Romans 8:6).

We are called children of God in Romans 8:14. *"For all who are being led by the Spirit of God, these are sons and daughters of God."* Children inherit from their parents. If we are children of God, it means we are also heirs of God. If we are heirs of God, we will inherit from God (Romans 8:14). What will we inherit?

We will inherit an eternal life in Christ Jesus. Christ is God's Son and heir. If we are children of God, then we are a brother with Christ and share in the same inheritance.

Paul ends with wonderful words to always remember: *"For I am convinced that neither death, nor life, nor angels, nor principalities, nor things present, nor things to come, nor powers, nor height, nor depth, nor any other created thing, will be able to separate us from the love of God, which is in Christ Jesus our Lord"* (Romans 8:38-39). Nothing can separate us from Christ. No sin you have committed can ever make Christ turn His back on you.

Things to Think On:

1. Do you feel you have a positive outlook on life or a negative one? If you seem to have a negative focus, how can you invite God to change it?

   _____

   _____

   _____

   _____

   _____

   _____

   _____

   _____

   _____

2. How do we know we belong to Christ? Hint: look at Romans 8:9.

   _____

   _____

   _____

   _____

_____

_____

_____

_____

_____

3. Does Romans 8:38-39 bring you
    comfort or concern? Why do you
    think this is the case? What is God
    speaking to you through your
    response?

    _____

    _____

    _____

    _____

    _____

    _____

    _____

    _____

    _____

    _____

    _____

4. Write out one verse that stood out
   to you from Romans Chapter 8.

   _____

   _____

   _____

   _____

   _____

Chapter 9

Faith in God is the key to making one right with God. But what does it mean? Just this: God's plan for all people is perfect and just. We have already discussed this to some extent. The last verse in chapter nine sums it up well. Trust in Christ means one will ever be disgraced (Romans 9:33).

God is a fair God. Romans 9:14 tells us *this very thing*. Paul reminds us there is no injustice with God. If there is no injustice, one can assume there is only justice. If there is justice from God, then it must be deserving. We have already established that God's will is perfect so it cannot be anything else.

God is also merciful and compassionate (Romans 9:15-16). These two attributes are not dependent on our actions. God Himself tells us *this very thing*. Paul is quoting from Exodus 33:19 in these two verses in Romans.

The words spoken come directly from God. He told Moses *this very thing* after Moses had gone up Mt. Sinai to receive the Ten Commandments from the Lord only to return to find the people had created a golden calf to worship instead of worshiping God. God was angry and Moses was interceding for the people.

This is a good reminder that no matter what our actions are, it is up to God to have mercy on us. We can only pray and ask for it. Nothing else will do.

Paul ends the chapter with another reminder from the Old Testament. This time he is quoting verses from the book of Isaiah (Isaiah 8:14, 28:16), which tell us trusting in Christ means one will never be disgraced.

Our faith and belief in Christ will always win out over anything which happens here on earth. Our eternal life is secure forever once we truly believe.

Things to Think On:

1. Have you ever felt like God has failed you? Confess it to Him now and pray about your response.

   _____

   _____

   _____

   _____

   _____

   _____

   _____

   _____

   _____

   _____

   _____

   _____

2. Re-read Romans 9:19-23. It's hard to view God through a lens of humanity. He sees all, knows all, and is

everywhere. We can't even begin to understand how God works. Write out Romans 9:22-23 as a reminder to trust God. _____

_____

_____

_____

_____

_____

_____

_____

_____

3. Do you ever depend on yourself too much to get things done? Do you stress and worry over your plans in life? Take some time to write out what you'd like to accomplish and then pray about it. Listen for God's answer. It may come immediately or

take time. Be open to whatever it is whenever it comes.

_____

_____

_____

_____

_____

_____

_____

_____

_____

4. Write out one verse that stood out to you from Romans Chapter 9.

_____

_____

_____

_____

Chapter 10

Paul begins to lay out God's plan for salvation in this chapter. He wants to ensure that everyone who hears the call and understands it will know how to answer it when it comes.

Now remember, Paul was once known as Saul and he persecuted Jews who had converted to "the Way" since the teachings of Christ did not line up with what Paul had been taught growing up. (Read the book of Acts to learn more about his conversion story). Jesus' miraculous touch on his life converted him into a zealous Christian. Paul was one who faced many trials and tribulations throughout his life once he gave up control to Christ, but he never wavered in telling others about Christ.

Paul is writing this letter to the Jews living in Rome. These are Jews who know the

Old Testament Scriptures as well as Paul. They were people who grew up memorizing the words of Moses and more. They were people who knew they were the chosen people of God and banked on that alone for their salvation. They were the same Jews who didn't recognize Jesus when He came to earth.

Paul certainly had his work cut out for him. It's one reason he quotes from the Old Testament so much. These same Jews knew those Scriptures. They knew of the prophesied coming of Christ. He used this knowledge to show them what had already happened. Christ had come and they had missed it.

He reminds them of God's righteousness in verse three of chapter ten. He tells them how the law of righteousness was removed for everyone who believes in Christ in verse four. He is laying the foundation here for how to have true salvation. Not one they thought would be given to them by birth, but one that is given to everyone who believes.

Then he gives it to them straight. In verses nine and ten he lays it out clearly *"…that if you confess with your mouth Jesus as Lord and believe in your heart that God raised Him from the dead, you will be saved; for with the heart a person believes, resulting in righteousness, and with the mouth he confesses, resulting in salvation."*

It really is that simple. If you confess you believe Jesus is Lord, you are a child of God. There is no special prayer you must say. There is no special ritual you must follow. You simply must confess your desire to live for Christ and not for yourself.

Things to Think On:

1. Have you done as verses nine and ten state? Have you confessed with your mouth that Jesus is Lord? If not, do it today! If so, remember the moment and the joy of your salvation! Write the date of your salvation (if you know it) or today's date (if today is the day!)

   _____

2. There are many Jews who think they will have eternal life simply because they are Jewish. This holds true for other denominations as well. What are your thoughts on this? Do you have a legacy of faith or do you have saving faith? What is the difference?

   _____

   _____

   _____

   _____

_____

_____

_____

_____

_____

_____

_____

3. As a Christian we are called to tell others about Jesus and there are many ways to accomplish this. Look at verse fifteen. How do you feel about this call to Christians? Are you living out this call in your life today? How could you do better?

_____

_____

_____

_____

_____

_____

_____

_____

_____

_____

_____

_____

_____

4. Write out one verse that stood out to you from Romans Chapter 10.

_____

_____

_____

_____

Chapter 11

Have you ever been angry at God because He didn't do what you thought He should? How often have you questioned His answers?

As human beings, we want to feel a sense of justice when something happens that has wronged us. We often forget that God is so much bigger. He sees all, knows all, understands all. It is unfathomable to us what He is capable of and, as humans, we often forget this due to our earthly sight rather than heavenly a sight.

Some of my favorite verses can be found in Romans 11:36-37.

Oh, the depth of the riches both of the wisdom
and knowledge of God!
How unsearchable are His judgements
and unfathomable His ways!

For who has known the mind of the Lord,
or who became His counselor?
Or who has first given to Him that it
might be paid back to him again?

For from Him and through Him and
to Him are all things.
To Him be the glory forever.
Amen.

These verses should bring comfort. God has wisdom and knowledge to a depth we can never know nor understand. Honestly, would we want to? What a burden it would be!

God is not only wise, but He is also gracious. It tells us in verse five as well as other places throughout the Scriptures. God's grace is so vast there is no way we could ever understand it all.

After all, it is through God's grace for us that He sent His son Jesus to die for our sins. Look back at Romans 5:15 and see what it has to say about this gift.

"But the free gift is not like the transgression.
For if by the transgression of the one the many died,
much more did the grace of God and the gift
by the grace of the one Man,
Jesus Christ abound to the many."

God's gift of grace is more than we could ever hope for or want for ourselves. Such a gift to those so undeserving is unimaginable, which makes it all the more precious.

Things to Think On:

1. List a few other verses from scripture telling of God's graciousness or grace.   If you don't have any committed to memory, do an internet search of "Scriptures about grace." Write down the ones that are most meaningful to you.

_____

_____

_____

_____

_____

_____

_____

_____

_____

_____

_____

_____

_____

2. Make a list of all the things making you think yourself undeserving of God's gift to you. Once you are done, cross each one out and write the word "grace" in big, bold, dark letters over your list as a reminder of God's perfect gift.

_____

_____

_____

_____

_____

_____

_____

_____

_____

_____

_____

_____

_____

_____

3. How do you feel knowing God is perfect and wise and knows exactly what you need each and every day? Write a thank you letter to God.

_____

_____

_____

_____

_____

_____

_____

_____

_____

_____

_____

_____

_____

_____

_____

_____

4. Write out one verse that stood out to you from Romans Chapter 11.

_____

_____

_____

_____

Chapter 12

J ustice. It's something we all want in life. Just turn on the news or go on social media and you will see people crying out for justice all over the place.

Romans chapter twelve takes our human need for justice and shows us what it looks like to truly mean it. Paul begins right away with verse two: *"And do not be conformed to this world..."* How often do we let the world dictate what we think or do? Our actions should always and only be backed by what *Scripture* tells us to do. Scripture is the yardstick we must use.

The reasoning is also shown in verse two: *"...so that you may prove what the will of God is, that which is good and acceptable and perfect."* How freeing it is to look at those words! We don't have to figure this life out. We simply need to live a life proving the will of God for our lives. When we do that, it is good and acceptable and even perfect to Him. I don't know about you, but this just blows my mind to think about.

Now back to the concept of justice. When we are wronged or see a wrong or feel something isn't "fair," what is our first thought almost every time? We want to make it right. We want to fix the wrong. We want it to be fair.

When we instead have our focus on Christ and what His will is for our life, we live a life which looks different from what the world considers "normal." Paul digs into this concept beginning with verse fourteen. This is what God has to say about justice.

In particular look at verses seventeen to nineteen: "*Never pay back evil for evil to anyone. Respect what is right in the sight of all men. If possible, so far as it depends on you, be at peace with all men. Never take your own revenge, beloved, but leave room for the wrath of God, for it is written, 'Vengeance is Mine, I will repay,' says the Lord."*

This is the type of upside-down life we live when we first focus on God and His will for our lives. Chapter twelve ends with the wisest words of all, *"Do not be overcome by evil, but overcome evil with good."*

Things to Think On:

1. What do you think about overcoming evil with good rather than looking for "pay back"? What other verses say a similar thing? Search them out (search the phrase "overcome evil") and write them down.

_____

_____

_____

_____

_____

_____

_____

_____

_____

_____

_____

_____

_____

_____

2. How can you overcome evil with good? What concrete steps of "goodness" can you take in a situation which seems unfair or unjust? How can you be a reflection of God's grace?

_____

_____

_____

_____

_____

_____

_____

_____

_____

_____

_____

_____

_____

_____

_____

_____

3. What are some things you can do to help you not "conform to the world"? Make a list you can refer to when you need a reminder.

_____

_____

_____

_____

_____

_____

_____

_____

4. Write out one verse that stood out to you from Romans Chapter 12.

_____

_____

_____

_____

Chapter 13

In Matthew 23 beginning in verse 36, we learn what the greatest commandments hinge on: love. We are told to love God with all of our heart, soul, and mind. We are also told to love our neighbors.

Paul reiterates this now in chapter thirteen when he tells the Romans to *"owe nothing to anyone except to love one another."* How simple yet how profound.

We often forget this in our day to day lives. We are striving after things of this world as we discussed in the last chapter. We forget we are to only strive after the things of Christ and to show love, Christ's self-sacrificial love, to those around us.

It seems so many people in the world have forgotten this. Simply scroll through your social media of choice and you will see post after post of people forgetting what loving others like Christ should look like. If we love like Christ, we won't break commandments like "don't commit adultery" or "you must not murder" or "you must not steal." If we are loving our neighbors like ourselves, those things won't even cross our minds. And if they do cross our minds, we are quick to ask for God's help to get past them.

Simple yet so very difficult to do. However, it's when we stop and look at the simple that we realize how difficult it can actually be. It's when we forget how we can't do this alone. We need help. We need some God-sized help to do this right.

God loves well. He loves perfectly. He loves with no mistakes. He loves despite our shortcomings. Love is the epitome of who God truly is. Without love, we can't ever know God fully. Without love we can't live our lives the way we should. I don't know about you, but the thought of this frightens me just a little.

If we live our lives striving after this perfect love lived out in our lives, we will be successful. Will it look perfect? Absolutely not. The only perfect person to have ever successfully lived a life of perfect love is Jesus Christ.

We are called to imitate His life with our own. We are called to live and love imperfectly through a perfect God.

Things to Think On:

1. Is there someone in your life right now that you need help loving self-sacrificially with God's help? Write out a prayer asking for just that.

    _____

    _____

    _____

    _____

    _____

    _____

    _____

    _____

    _____

    _____

    _____

2. Do you find yourself drawn into social media and the pain and suffering seemingly happening all the time in the world? The next time this

happens stop and pray. Ask for God to help you see the situation through His eyes.

_____

_____

_____

_____

_____

_____

_____

_____

_____

_____

_____

3. How can you show God's love to those around you? Brainstorm some specific ideas. Start with your loved ones and extend to those you have a tough time loving well. Have a plan for a situation you've struggled with

in the past so when the opportunity
next arises, you will be ready to show
God's love.

_____

_____

_____

_____

_____

_____

_____

_____

_____

_____

4. Write out one verse that stood out to
you from Romans Chapter 13.

_____

_____

_____

_____

Chapter 14

Do you find people spend a lot of time judging others for their actions or their speech or their clothes or fill in the blank. Do you?

No one likes to be judged. I know I certainly don't and I'm sure you are the same. There are various verses throughout the Scriptures speaking about this very thing.

Paul addresses it here in Romans chapter fourteen starting in verse thirteen. However, verse thirteen starts with the word *therefore* so let's back up a moment to look at what it says before that.

Why does Paul tell us not to judge one another? Verse twelve gives us the answer: *"So then each one of us will give an account of himself to God."* We are not to judge others because we will one day be judged ourselves. God will be the ultimate and final judge and we need to remember it.

Backing up a little bit more, why is Paul addressing this here and now in this chapter? It seems like the Romans were having issues with each other in the normal things they were doing. They were causing each other to question their dedication to living a life for Christ.

This is what Paul is addressing in this chapter. There are many things in the world that are not sinful, yet some people feel they are, for example drinking alcohol. You may not feel this is a sin. However, if someone you know *does* consider it a sin, then you need to look at how your actions may cause them to stumble. Paul tells it plainly in verse thirteen. We should not "*put an obstacle or a stumbling block in a brother's way.*"

Remember back in chapter thirteen we discussed love and what it looks like. This is another way of loving your neighbors.

The bottom line here is simply this, if you consider yourself a Christian, be careful how you present yourself to the world. We all know the person who has a Christian fish symbol on the back of their car and yet won't hesitate to cut you off in traffic. Or, we know a Christian parent attending a ballgame who offers their player degradation instead of encouragement.

Consider how someone who was spiritually searching, or a new Christian, might view this person and thus Jesus Christ through their actions. *That* is what Paul is getting to here. Our actions should always reflect Christ. Always.

Things to Think On:

1. What is one thing you find yourself judging on a regular basis? What is one thing you can do to remind yourself not to or to pray in that situation? Work on creating a new habit.

   _____

   _____

   _____

   _____

   _____

   _____

   _____

2. Do you do things that others might consider "un-Christian?" Consider changing your behavior(s) to better reflect Christ.

   _____

   _____

_____

_____

_____

_____

_____

_____

_____

3. How does knowing God will one day judge all of mankind impact you today? Will you change anything about how you live your life in view of eternity?

_____

_____

_____

_____

_____

_____

_____

_____

_____

_____

_____

_____

4. Write out one verse that stood out to
   you from Romans Chapter 14.

   _____

   _____

   _____

   _____

   _____

Chapter 15

It's easy to fall prey to the things of the world which steal joy and peace and hope. They are everywhere and seem to be growing by the day if not the hour. This is just where the evil one wants you, hopeless and despairing, feeling like there is no joy in the world at all.

Paul, however, tells us how to counteract those feelings. Remember, there is "nothing new under the sun" as it says over and over in the book of Ecclesiastes. God has been around for a long time. For all time, really. The things that were happening in Paul's day are happening now. Life isn't much different in terms of human behavior from millennia ago to the present day.

Yet in about the middle of chapter fifteen we learn something that will help us build a hedge against despair and hopelessness. Read verse thirteen out loud: *"Now may the God of hope fill you with all joy and peace in believing, so that you will abound in hope by the power of the Holy Spirit."* If you are working on memorizing verses from Romans, I highly recommend this one.

Why does God want to fill us with all joy and peace? I love watching for the two small words *"so that"* in Scripture. Paul tells us exactly why he wants this for the church in Rome. He wants God to fill them with all joy and peace *"so that you will abound in hope by the power of the Holy Spirit."* This makes my heart sing when I read it and think deeply on just those words.

God wants what is good for us all the time. What is good for us? Hope in Him. Why hope? Because the ultimate product of having hope in God is joy and peace in all things. And how can we have this joy and peace and hope? Through the power of the Holy Spirit.

Will hope in God make the world less evil? Unfortunately, no. It will, however, help us to see things through God's eyes and not our human eyes. The world will never be fixed the way we think it should until Jesus Christ one day returns. What a glorious day that will be! It will only be then that evil will be vanquished, and true joy and peace and hope will be victorious.

Things to Think On:

1. What is one thing you can do today to help lessen the amount of despair in your life? Is it turning off the news? Less time on social media? Consider deeply the things that will help you find more joy and peace in Christ. Make a list to refer to when you are feeling more hopelessness than hope.

_____

_____

_____

_____

_____

_____

_____

_____

_____

_____

_____

_____

2. Consider starting a "gratitude journal" where you record the good things in life from the simple to the profound. What's one thing you are grateful for today?

    _____

    _____

    _____

    _____

    _____

    _____

    _____

3. God is the God of peace (Romans 15:33). Reflect on what that means to you. Write the verse out here.

    _____

    _____

    _____

    _____

    _____

4. Write out one verse that stood out to you from Romans Chapter 15.

_____

_____

_____

_____

_____

_____

Chapter 16

You may feel this last chapter of Romans had little to say about who God is or about His character. This is the conclusion of Paul's letter to the Romans and he is spending some time here naming and thanking specific people, but there are some things still to be gleaned about God in this last chapter.

We learn three things about God which are important to remember in the last few verses. We learn He is the God of peace (Romans 16:20), as mentioned in the last chapter. We also learn He is eternal (Romans 16:26) and He is wise (Romans 16:27).

Why do these two things matter when we are looking at the character of God? Paul tells us why in verse twenty-five. He tells the Romans the reason for writing this letter and for telling others about Christ is simply this, they need to share the *"revelation of the mystery which has been kept secret for long ages past."* In other words, they need to spread the good news of Jesus Christ to those around them.

We are still called to this day to do the same. Are we called to be an apostle like Paul? Maybe. Maybe not. However, as a Christian our one goal in life should be to tell others about the saving grace of Jesus and how they can know *"the only wise God, through Jesus Christ"* (Romans 16:27).

Often, I think we say to ourselves, "someone else will do it" or "that's not my calling" or "I couldn't possibly know what to say" or even "what if they ask me a question I can't answer." All of these are due to one thing and one thing only, fear. We must fear God more than we fear people and failure. We must obey God more than we let fear rule our actions.

Remember, we serve an eternal God full of peace, hope, love, and joy. A God with these character traits can take away any fear we may feel. Trust Him fully. Ask Him to help you overcome any fear you may have of telling His good news to others. Ask for the opportunities and the strength and the words. He will always supply them.

Things to Think On:

1. What are the fears holding you back the most from telling others about Christ? Write them out and ask God to help you overcome it.

   _____

   _____

   _____

   _____

   _____

   _____

   _____

   _____

   _____

2. If you don't have a fear about sharing about Christ, write out what you would tell someone else facing that fear. How did you overcome it?

   _____

   _____

   _____

_____

_____

_____

_____

_____

_____

3. What are your final thoughts on the
   book of Romans? What was your
   favorite thing you gleaned from this
   study? Which was your favorite
   memory verse and why?

   _____

   _____

   _____

   _____

   _____

   _____

   _____

   _____

   _____

4. Write out one verse that stood out to you from Romans Chapter 16.

_____

_____

_____

_____

_____

_____

_____

Conclusion

I pray you enjoyed this study of the Book of Romans. I would encourage you to continue reading and studying God's Word. There is much to be learned about the character of God and how we can relate to Him throughout the Scriptures.

For the report of your obedience has reached to all;
therefore I am rejoicing
over you, but I want you to be wise
in what is good and innocent in what is evil.
The God of peace will soon crush Satan under your
feet.
The grace of our Lord Jesus be with you.
Romans 16:19-20

Acknowledgments

This study is a direct result of a class I took through New England Bible College. "Topics in the Bible: The Epistle to the Romans" was taught the spring of 2020 at Fayette Baptist Church by Dr. Samuel Caldwell. His enthusiasm and passion for the topic showed through in all he shared. It has, hands down, been the best class I've taken thus far through this college.

Thank you also to my wonderful friend, Molly Sparling, who went through and helped me tweak and make this study better. Any errors are mine alone.

Thank you to my hubby for once more reading and proofing something I've written. At least this time it wasn't a romance story. Thanks, honey.

I do not consider myself a Bible scholar in any way. I pray this study helps you use the best resource there is for learning more about God and His plan for your life: the Bible. Read it daily. Pray daily. Learn to listen to His urgings on your life and obey.

About the Author

Lisa-Anne Berry is a wife and mother who desires to learn more about God daily. She lives in rural Maine with her husband of twenty-seven years and their three rapidly growing boys. After homeschooling all three of their sons, Lisa-Anne has started embarking on the next chapter of her life, becoming an author. Her fiction titles can be found under the pen name of Evelyn Grace. When not writing, she can be found curled up with a hot mug of tea, a book, and her slightly fluffy kitty named Maggie.

Made in the USA
Las Vegas, NV
06 November 2023

80368659R00069